Conduct

Becoming

A Man

Handbook

On How to Behave and Why

J. Allen Hood

CONDUCT BECOMING

A Man Handbook

On How to Behave and Why

Copyright © 2017 J. Allen Hood
All rights reserved.
Published by Snakes & Snails Publishing 2019
Las Vegas, NV, USA

Cover Design J. Allen Hood

ISBN-13: 978-1-7335245-0-6

For Conner, Jett, James, Karsten, Konrad and Kornel.

FIRST...THE BAD STUFF

NOW...THE NORMAL STUFF

FINALLY...THE GOOD STUFF

This isn't the "how to be happy" handbook.

Life is full of failure and frustration and it's a pretty safe bet there's plenty of bad times ahead.

This book outlines a path through all that, a code of conduct developed over countless generations. The man's way.

I'm not going to lie to you — it isn't the path of least resistance. It's the harder road with delayed reward.

Half of us are born male, yet no one is born a man. It takes effort and determination. You don't luck into it, you can't buy it and it doesn't matter who your dad is. You decide to conduct yourself a certain way. You take the hard right over the easy wrong. You earn it.

Ultimately, you may decide manhood, as described inside, is not for you. Humans are complicated, and what fills one may leave another empty.

So, read the book. Think about it, then choose.

J. Allen Hood

Handbook Primer

Many books on "how to be a man," "manhood" and "manliness" deal with the physical. They cover skills and actions. How to do things like tie knots, ride motorcycles or chop down trees.

This handbook is different. It's about dealing with the key human being in your life — you. It covers the mental aspect of manhood.

After all, being you is all in your head.

So, let's start with one basic fact.

When dealing with people, yourself included, the most important word to remember is…

Influence: *the act or power of producing an effect without apparent exertion of force or direct exercise of command.*

The significant part of this definition is "without apparent exertion of force."

When you think about it, life is you interacting with the world.

When you interact with objects, you use physical force; you swing a hammer, type on a keyboard or put on your pants. You perform an action to accomplish a task.

If you want to build a house — you use force. Go to a concert — also force. Get groceries — force. You have one choice.

When you interact with people, you have two choices: force or influence. Force comes from your body, influence from your mind.

If you're strong enough, you can use your body to force people to do what you want. That's only acceptable to defend, rescue or protect. Outside of that, forcing others to do what you want is the worst method. It's generally immoral and often illegal. It's the method of last resort.

When you put it in these terms, you realize many of your interactions with people are actually contests of influence. You're trying to get them to do what you want. They're doing the same.

It helps to put these "contests" in proper perspective. To do that, consider the intent behind them.

When you influence people for their benefit, it's motivation.

When you influence people for your benefit, it's manipulation.

Of course, there are degrees. "Hey, can you hand me that hammer?" is manipulating you to my benefit, but it's not the same as "Hey, you should give me your car."

As the methods are often the same, it's the intent that determines if it's a good (moral) or bad (immoral) act.

A drill sergeant yelling at you may seem cruel, but his intent is motivation. The drill sergeant is getting nothing out of the exchange. Only you benefit. He's teaching you, that with proper motivation you can accomplish more than you think. A sports coach does the same thing.

If you can't figure out why someone is doing something, ask yourself…

"Who benefits?"

And...

"Is this person smart enough to be doing this for a reason?" Or, do you imagine he hasn't thought it through at all?

A person trying to motivate you seldom hides it. He may not tell you outright, but it should be easy to see. The harder it is to figure out a person's motive, the more likely he's trying to manipulate you.

Take this book for example: I can't force you to handle life's challenges like a man. This handbook is my attempt to influence you.

So,

"Who benefits?"

And...

"Is he smart enough to be doing it for a reason?"

Prologue — Before You Begin
Why?

"For the strength of the pack is the wolf, and the strength of the wolf is the pack."

- The Law for the Wolves. Rudyard Kipling

Why did I write this? More importantly, why bother reading it, let alone put in the effort required to become the man I'll describe?

In the wild, if the pack is going to prosper, the wolves must cooperate. They must trust each other to behave a certain way.

As social animals, humans are the same. In a survival situation, each man must conduct himself "a man among men" if the tribe is to prosper.

Men follow a code. Following the code allows them to recognize one another. This plants the seeds of trust needed for cooperation.

The basic rules...

> **You will fight for the tribe** — to your death if required — to protect the women and children.

> **You will be honest with the tribe** so good decisions can be made. Decisions should be based on facts. If there is dishonesty, plans fail.

> **You will do what you say**. The tribe is counting on you. If you don't deliver, the tribe suffers. You become part of the problem.

The various cultural codes of manhood (samurai bushido and knight chivalry, as examples) all grew out of the above philosophy.

Historically, the code of manhood was enforced. It was necessary. Men who failed to live up to the basic rules couldn't be trusted so they were either killed or cast off.

However, as societies grew they became more efficient, developing tools and methods that increased safety and prosperity. The wheel and sail advanced trade. Ranching and farming provided a steady food supply. Knowledge spread through the written word.

Finally, the invention of the gun made men and women equally dangerous. Now both sexes could readily kill to protect themselves and their children.

With all these advances, the value of the code began to diminish. As its value diminished, the need to enforce the code went with it.

Today, it's unnecessary to kill or banish those who don't follow the code. If your neighbor is a liar and a coward, it's unlikely to cause you harm. So, we tolerate it.

Given all this, why should you be any different?

That's truly up to you.

When tough times arrive, and they always do, humanity still calls upon the men — those who adhere to the code.

Do you want to be among them, or would you rather watch.

FIRST...THE BAD STUFF

Weakness

Everyone is born weak; physically, mentally and morally.

Physical strength is the ability to apply force. It is developed through resistance training — lifting weights, calisthenics and similar exercise. Physical strength is self-explanatory and there's a lot of information available on the internet, so research workout routines and strength training.

Mental strength is the ability to positively *influence* yourself. I'm talking about determination, self-discipline and courage. Examples include; resisting the temptation to eat more chips, attempting something you've never done before or pushing yourself when you feel like quitting. It's the willingness to pay the hard price, and the ability to overcome your fears.

Moral strength is social teamwork, the measure other men use to decide whether they want you in their tribe. It's refusing to maintain or improve your position at the expense of another person or the truth. An example would be owning up to a mistake that will probably get you in trouble.

Mental and moral strength are the main elements of one's character. I imagine you've heard that before, in context with enduring something difficult or facing a setback, followed with the wisdom that, "it isn't all bad, it builds character!" It actually does.

Understand everything you do gets easier over time, and this works both ways. If you give in to temptation once, you're likely to give in again. If you surrender to weakness, the weakness grows. If you resist, it's you who grows.

Resist. If you don't, it becomes increasingly difficult to overcome these patterns of weakness. Do this long enough and you end up human garbage — dangerous to yourself and those around you.

Imagine if a physically weak person must lift something to free someone trapped, or if a mentally weak person must summon the courage to confront a violent attacker. Or, imagine a morally weak person ending up in a position of power. The end result is the same — failure.

FIRST...THE BAD STUFF

Bad things happen when weak people end up in challenging situations. Regardless of their intentions, they often fail and end up hurting others.

This leads back to the old lie, "Well, at least they meant well, at least they tried." That's bullshit.

At the end of the day, results count, intentions don't. There's no place in the world of men for best intentions. If you intend to build a flying machine, you better build and test it before offering a ride. Telling the other guy, "well, at least I tried," as he plummets to his death offers little consolation. It's criminal.

It's difficult to be strong throughout your life, but it does get easier. Life's many challenges will provide the resistance you need to grow physically, mentally and morally strong.

Welcome these challenges. You can't grow without them.

FIRST...THE BAD STUFF

FIRST…THE BAD STUFF

Fear

Everyone is afraid at various points in their lives. Don't believe anyone telling you differently.

People generally hide their fear. But you should know if you're afraid of something, most others are too.

Courage is the mental strength to go ahead in the face of that fear.

Cowardice is letting that fear overwhelm you.

When you're young it's common to be afraid, because many things are unknown. Without experience, you don't know what to do or what to expect. You have no idea just how dangerous or difficult something is.

As you grow older and gain experience, you become less fearful. You'll have either done it before or done something similar, and the more often you do something, the less frightening it becomes.

FIRST...THE BAD STUFF

Before I go further, to properly deal with fear, it helps to understand your body's reaction. So, I'm going to briefly touch on the science.

You may know the feeling of fear is actually your body dumping adrenaline into your bloodstream. This has a number of physical effects.

This is the "fight or flight" instinct you've heard about. It happens when your mind recognizes something as dangerous. This could be an action you are about to attempt, an attacking person or animal; anything you think could harm you.

Being afraid of heights is a good example. Your mind tells your body: "If you fall from here, you'll probably die."

In Airborne school (Army paratrooper school) they make the training obstacles different heights to maximize this response. These obstacles are designed to scare you — so you learn to overcome fear. If fear paralyzes you or makes you quit, you become less than useless. You become a danger to those around you.

During an adrenaline dump your lungs process air better and your heart pumps faster, providing extra energy for your muscles and brain. Your pupils dilate so details improve, but this causes parts of your eye to temporarily burn out due to too much light, so you also get tunnel vision.

Basically, your blood leaves the organs you're not going to be using and concentrates on the organs you'll need to either fight or run away.

If someone was incapable of fear, he'd never get this adrenaline "turbo boost," putting him at a physical disadvantage.

So fear isn't bad, it's all in how you handle it.

The key is to recognize the adrenaline dump for what it is, then work through it while keeping your wits. A person with a clear head is working at greater efficiency than someone who either didn't have an adrenaline dump or can't think clearly while it's happening.

Now, it's certainly OK to act like you're not afraid. In fact, you should. It helps you control yourself and get back to thinking straight.

The bravest soldiers often admit to their buddies they were afraid — after the fact. They won't discuss it while it's happening. And because fear can be contagious, they won't show it. If you talk about it, others may start thinking about their own fear, which can cause them to quit.

As a paratrooper in the Army, I jumped out of airplanes. I was afraid of heights and still am. I was afraid during training and every time we went up for a jump.

I did it anyway.

I recognized what I was feeling was fear, decided I was committed to doing it, and put the fear aside. Even though the fear remained, it became easier every time.

An interesting side note about fear: After it's all over, you'll feel really good, another byproduct of adrenaline. This feeling causes some people to become adrenaline junkies.

They like it so much they put themselves in dangerous situations just to get that rush.

However, if you aren't an adrenaline junkie, the more time you have to think about something frightening, the greater the likelihood you won't do it. The fear builds up inside you — so don't overthink it.

Which leads to one more thing:

Leading up to a fight, if your opponent is afraid and he sees you are, too, he'll focus on your fear. He'll exaggerate the threat or make fun of you. Dragging it out. Building your fear. Hoping you'll quit.

If you quit first, then he can quit, too, and not look like a coward. He set you up for that. He effectively hid his own fear by creating a courage contest, and you lost.

I'll go more into this in the section on fighting, but it plays a big part in all the shit-talking people do.

You must recognize your fear. Understand it, then set it aside. Don't dwell on it. Don't keep thinking about it.

Make your decision. Either do it or don't. If you find yourself scared in the middle, stop thinking and fully commit — if you quit in the middle, you get the worst result.

So, either quit before you start or go all the way. Those are your choices.

Bullying

Bullies target people afraid to fight or talk back, so fear and bullying go hand-in-hand.

Schoolyard bullies are cowards at heart. So, there's always going to be something about the target that says, "This person is safe to pick on." But the bully still tests first, just to make sure.

Potential victims seem like safe targets when the bully doesn't see them as social or physical threats.

There's no physical threat when the bully thinks the target doesn't have the courage to fight back. Or, in the rare case they may fight, the bully is confident he can beat them easily.

Being a social threat is more complicated.

First, the victim can't be popular. No one picks on the guy everybody likes.

He also can't be in a social group known for violence. Bullies aren't going to pick on someone with buddies who like to fight (this creates an indirect physical threat).

Finally, the target isn't known as a good shit-talker, so the bully doesn't have to worry about getting verbally humiliated.

Besides not being a social or physical threat, a few other factors go into target selection.

Even if the bully is bigger and stronger, something about the target threatens the bully's ego. The target can do something well, so the bully feels the need to prove himself.

The target might be a good artist, skilled gamer or play guitar. A teacher might compliment their intelligence. A pretty girl may like them.

All these things could highlight a shortcoming within the bully. He's not an artist or musician. The teacher never compliments him. The pretty girl never notices. So, he bullies to get his power back—to make himself feel better.

(While I have used "he" to describe a bully, bullying is not exclusive to males. A female bully can be even more challenging, because it's socially unacceptable for a male victim to respond to any physical threat.)

Another reason people bully is to establish the dominance order within a group. This is often referred to as "the pecking order." The term came from people noticing chickens will peck inferior chickens and allow themselves to be pecked by superiors.

If there's a new guy in the group and there's a question about who outranks who, you may see some bullying. This normally stops once the order is settled, only coming back up if the order slips.

Dogs do the same thing, which is one reason they fight. Both feel they should be top dog, so they snap at each other until one backs down.

Unfortunately, people often make these situations worse. Well-meaning people alter the natural order within a group. This confuses everyone, and fighting can result.

"Water finds its own level" means the natural order will eventually work itself out. But disturbing it out of good intentions often has a negative result.

An example: In a home, if the small dog is constantly praised and the large dog punished, the small dog might get the impression it is top dog in the pack.

If this confusion exists, and the small dog challenges the large dog when the owner isn't home, the large dog may attack and kill the small dog to fix the pecking order.

Another thing that can be confusing, bullying from a position of strength — where the bully is clearly superior. In this scenario, what appears to be bullying sometimes isn't. It's negative encouragement.

Consider the Army drill sergeant.

Obviously, drill sergeants aren't threatened by privates. Yet they bully privates without mercy. It's apparent they aren't doing it to feel superior — in the Army, they clearly are. Then why do they do it?

They do it to test, and if it's needed, to toughen the privates up. They want to see if the privates will cry and stop trying, flip out and quit or stop being part of the team. All these things are bad. They want to identify anyone prone to these behaviors and eliminate their weakness.

You see the same thing with groups of male friends. They test and tease each other. It's natural and acceptable, as long as no one gets injured. However, they need to make sure other people don't see the roasting and take it the wrong way. (So, don't tease your friends in front of people who may not get it.)

The best way to deal with a bully? Never come off like a safe target in the first place. Don't look weak. Don't show fear.

If you find yourself the target of bullying, take action or it'll only get worse.

First you need to understand what the bully is trying to do and why. Do you threaten his ego in some way? Why? Is he doing it to tease you, to establish a pecking order, or to negatively encourage you? Figure it out.

At its roots, bullying is social. Bullies get their courage from the audience — remember this. It helps when trying to figure out the why. Who's the audience?

In almost every case, a bully starts by testing to see what you'll do. Will you back down? Will you laugh it off? Will you stand there and take it? Pass this test and the bullying stops before it ever really gets started.

If you prove you won't quit and can give as good as you get, he'll leave you alone. If he realizes you're a social or physical threat, you're not worth the risk.

If, after all this, the bullying continues, the best course of action is to handle it on your own.

If you get someone else involved, you fail the test and the bully will go after you as soon as he thinks it's safe.

In the case of establishing an order, if another party comes in and fixes it, you now have a situation like I described with the dogs. Eventually if there is a fight, it'll be worse.

Because bullies derive their power from an audience, if you can confront the bully alone, you may be able to talk it out. Fair warning: Don't try this unless you're prepared to fight.

If you can't resolve it by talking and you must fight, it's better to fight a bully when he doesn't have friends around. His friends will give him courage and may help him if you start to win.

A coward never fights alone, so if you're willing to fight it may scare the living shit out of him. This gives you an edge in any fight.

When you're young, dealing with a bully can be a challenge. But if you want to become a man, you need to handle it. And once you start showing the basics of manhood, you'll find the bullies all gradually disappear.

FIRST…THE BAD STUFF

Fighting

Fear, bullying and fighting. As a boy, this is often the order of things; first one, then the next, and finally—a fight.

I'm not going into detail on the physical fundamentals of fighting. At a minimum you should learn how to strike, block and avoid a takedown. Find a way to take some self-defense classes if possible. If not, ask a friend or family member to teach you. If you can't do either, watch some videos and practice with friends.

You need to know the basics because there's a good chance you'll end up in a fight at some point. Don't worry, it's not the end of the world.

When you're young, one-on-one with no weapons involved, the damage will likely be minimal — even if you lose. However, if you don't fight, the damage to your self-esteem can be worse than any injury.

If you let fear get the better of you and back down, you'll start to hate yourself afterward, so you'll try to convince yourself you made the right choice.

If you made the right choice, you'll know. You won't spend time questioning it.

If you made the wrong choice, you'll question it over and over, trying to justify it in your mind. If you find yourself doing that, you made the wrong choice. Stop dwelling on it. Learn from it, then leave it in the past. Make the right choice next time.

The hardest thing about fighting is the initial adrenaline dump; it's that sudden fear when you realize a fight is about to kick-off. You'll worry about getting hurt. You'll worry about getting embarrassed. You'll think and think, getting more and more nervous.

This is when the shit-talking starts.

If the other person starts running his mouth it means he's afraid. Just as afraid as you, maybe more. He's trying to scare you, hoping you'll quit before the fight starts. Recognize this — he's playing you to hide his own fear.

If you know a fight's coming and you can't see a good way out, stop worrying and commit — 100%.

FIRST...THE BAD STUFF

If the other person punches or pushes you, the fight's started — join in. If you don't you'll get beat up, seriously embarrassed or both.

Damage to your face, bruises and black eyes, heals quickly. Damage to your mental strength however, is invisible and takes a long time to heal.

That kind of damage can change who you are and who you become. It can impact your confidence and limit your potential. People sense it and you might find yourself the target of bullying as a result.

When the fight starts, the decision to throw your first punch is the hardest. Once that punch is thrown, the fear changes into something else. Adrenaline is now on your side. Throw the punch, commit to the fight and you're guaranteed some form of victory.

If the other person was testing you, even if you fight and lose, you'll likely earn his respect. But more importantly, you'll earn self-respect.

If you fight and find yourself winning, you have a decision to make. When someone's at your mercy, you can either let up or continue.

Legally, once the other person stops fighting and the danger is over, any further action you take can get you in trouble. Just make sure you've definitely won. Don't allow him to get back up if there's still fight in him. If you're confident the fight's over, let up.

If you beat up someone in your social group, after the fight, let it go. In most cases he'll try to be your friend, or at a minimum, leave you alone. In fact, he'll often want to be your friend even if you lose! You've proved you can be counted on to fight. That's an important part of the man's code.

If you win, don't brag. You'll look petty. If he starts back up talking shit, which is rare, ignore him if possible. If not, confront him alone.

Outside of people you know, you can avoid most fights by paying attention and not being in the wrong place at the wrong time. If you see the potential for a fight developing, gather your friends and leave.

If some stranger starts threatening you, it's a test. Cowering or begging will give him courage, right when he's deciding how risky it'll be to fight you. That actually increases the chance he'll attack. If you look like you're ready to fight, he'll often just talk some shit and move on.

If you're attacked by surprise, fight back! Don't expect anyone to show you mercy. It never happens. Fighting back may force your attacker to rethink his plan, open a way to escape, or allow time for help to arrive.

There are some situations in life where there are just no good outcomes possible, only various levels of bad. Come to terms with this reality.

If you can't avoid these situations, you have some choices — none are good. Fight and win; maybe getting hurt in the process. Fight and lose; probably getting hurt in the process. Stand there and get your ass kicked.

Your call.

FIRST...THE BAD STUFF

Evil

There are very few truly evil people in civilized society. In day-to-day life, most "evil" people and most "evil" actions are just examples of mental and moral weakness.

People generally lie because they're too weak to admit the truth, not because they're deliberately trying to harm others. They lie to protect themselves from the consequences of their behavior.

Most people cheat on their lovers because they're unhappy, can't resist temptation or have weak egos that need reassurance. It's not because they want to hurt their partners.

One major reason people steal is because they've never developed the mental and moral strength to overcome life's obstacles and earn what they want through hard work.

Often murder is also the result of weakness; too weak to control their emotions, too weak to get something they want by honest means, too weak to resist the manipulation of another person (who is using the murderer either because he can't or is too smart to do it himself).

Observing an "evil" person will often reveal this underlying weakness. He'll focus solely on himself with no regard for others. He barely has the strength to help himself, let alone someone else, so he'll avoid challenging situations.

Don't confuse weakness with evil, doing that gives the weak too much credit. Pity them but don't fear them. Study their weakness so you can understand it, but don't tolerate their destructive behavior.

Finally, when you see mental or moral weakness in others, take note. Realize if situations come up that challenge those weaknesses, they'll probably fail.

Don't put your trust in weak people and hope for the best. You'll end up disappointed.

Lies

You've seen the negative impact of lies. You've lied. People have lied to you. It seldom works out.

Lying is often the quickest, yet almost always the worst, way out. People can't make good decisions based on lies. The facts are not, in fact, facts. Lies lead to bad decisions, bad decisions lead to bad results.

Besides being morally weak, lying for your own benefit is generally foolish. Sure, it allows you to avoid or hide something, but it doesn't actually fix anything.

If you're lucky, your lie will stay hidden forever. That seldom happens. The truth almost always comes out. Now, what started out as a situation so bad you felt compelled to lie, is worse. You have the original problem, plus the fact you're a liar and can't be trusted stacked on top.

On rare occasion, lying for someone else's benefit can be acceptable, but make sure it's truly for them and not just a way to make things easier on you.

Use this to judge: If I lie for this other person's benefit, will it make things harder for me? If the answer is yes, then — maybe.

Understand, at some point the truth may still come out, and your lie will have made things worse. "The road to hell is paved with good intentions." Get ready to pay the price if (or more likely, when) the lie blows up in your face. Remember, best intentions don't amount to shit in the real world.

The only time it's almost always OK to lie is when you're comforting a dying loved one. Hopefully, you won't have to deal with that any time soon.

You will make mistakes. Tell the truth and stand ready to pay the price. You'll impress men and women of character. You probably won't escape punishment, but you just may unlock a door somewhere in your future.

Secrecy

You don't have to share what you know with anyone, even if asked. Many things are best left unsaid.

Few secrets are positive in nature. It's generally gossip about someone's mistakes, poor judgment or failure. Unless you're trying to warn others, don't share people's shame with the world. Don't trade garbage.

The exception to this is abuse. If you or someone you know is being physically or sexually abused, you need to report it. Tell a parent or an authority figure you can trust.

Given your youth, when it comes to secrecy, you and your friends are in the same boat. Almost no one can keep a secret at any age, but young people are among the worst.

If secrecy is the water, trust is the glass. Be careful who you trust, or your secrets will get spilled all over the place. As you get older and have more life experience, you'll become a better judge of who you can and who you can't trust.

Nowadays people sue each other over anything, so running your mouth can get people in trouble. Keep that in mind before you discuss things which could potentially come back and hurt you or the people you care about.

Today, it's not uncommon for a girl to send you naked pictures of themselves. Be very careful with this. If she's under 18 you can get in trouble just by having them. If she's over 18, never post them online, email them or allow anyone else to have a copy. You can ruin someone's reputation, hurt them emotionally and get in legal trouble. There's nothing to gain and a lot to lose. Don't do it.

It's tempting to share secrets with people. This is because subconsciously, you're hoping to impress them with your knowledge or your access to other people's secrets.

You may not realize it, but you're also teaching them you can't keep a secret.

Would you tell a secret to someone who regularly told you other people's secrets? No. You'd be a fool if you did. He's already proven to you he'll turn around and tell others.

Loneliness

If you're the child of a single parent, you're probably alone more often than someone from a two-parent family. Even more so if you don't have brothers or sisters.

When you spend a lot of time alone, you end up with more time to think. It can be tempting to focus on the negatives in your life. Don't fall into this trap. It doesn't help and it won't fix anything. It only makes matters worse.

A better use of all this thinking time is to be creative. Think about the things you want to be, see and do. Then make a plan.

Decide which steps to take and start taking them. If you want to be anything more than a dreamer, you need to put down the phone and get off the couch. If you don't make the effort to fulfill your plans, you're the only one to blame.

I understand it's tempting to lose yourself in video games and online. This is OK, in moderation.

Today, social media and forums allow you to have conversations with people from all over the world. Use this to your advantage.

Seek out websites that discuss things you're interested in. Sports and video game sites are probably a given, but you'll likely be surrounded by the same type of people you know at school, so branch out.

If you're interested in something unusual like drones or computer building, find an online forum for that hobby. You can ask questions or learn a lot just reading other people's comments. If you find something particularly interesting, study it further.

Use the internet to learn as much as you can. The more you know, the more of life's puzzle pieces you have. When you don't know something, you're at the mercy of those who do.

At a minimum, get a basic understanding of math, electronics, physics, machines and people. You can figure out quite a bit just knowing these fundamentals. School should help with some of this stuff, but you'll need to supplement your education on your own.

A broad knowledge of the basics has another benefit: You can do a lot of things yourself. You won't have to pay people or ask for help. This is handy when you're starting out and don't have a lot of money.

Alone time is perfect for this kind of learning. It keeps your mind busy and gives you a sense of accomplishment. You also gain skills or knowledge that'll be useful down the road.

A word of caution: When visiting online forums and chat sites, don't let anyone convince you to provide personal information, photos or arrange to meet. There's no good reason for someone to ask, so if he keeps asking, report him to a forum moderator or someone you trust. Girls and young women are more likely to be approached than you, but it still happens. Use your head.

Besides video games, forums and social media, you also have other entertainment opportunities; TV, online videos, podcasts and books (written and audio). There's so much stuff it can keep you busy full time. Don't let it.

If you lose yourself entirely in screens, your social life and physical fitness will suffer. Make sure you leave time to do something social, like sports, a school hobby or an interest club.

Sitting in front of a glowing screen all the time makes you physically weak and socially awkward. If you have any interest in girls, this is a bad place to start.

Exercise is great because it works in two ways. It releases chemicals that improve your mood and it's a positive step towards other things that'll make your life better. You'll feel better, look better and gain confidence.

One last thought on alone time: You don't have to pretend everything in your life is awesome.

Undoubtedly your life isn't perfect, no one's is. Some people have it far better than you, but some have it far worse. Sitting around feeling sorry for yourself won't change anything.

Find something to take your mind off the negatives. Learn something new or exercise.

FIRST…THE BAD STUFF

Depression

If your life isn't progressing the way you'd like, figure out the reasons why, then change the things you can.

Don't get overwhelmed and frustrated by the things beyond your control. In one form or another, they're always going to be there.

As a minor, you can't change most aspects of your school and home life. Your family, teachers and fellow students — all are generally beyond your control. As you get older, this becomes your job, bosses and coworkers.

When you feel depressed, identify the things beyond your control and move past them. Don't dwell on them. Instead, take control of the things you can.

What you can control is how you react to things. React in a measured way. Think about what you're going to do before you do it.

If something bad happens, at the end of the day, think about it. Was there anything you could've done to change how things turned out? Sometimes the answer will be yes, sometimes no.

Be honest with yourself. If you mishandled a situation, learn from it. Tell yourself not to react that way again. If it truly was beyond your control, recognize there was nothing you could've done. Put it behind you.

Don't beat yourself up over things you can't control. In fact, don't beat yourself up over anything. Look inside, recognize when you fail, and change. Staying depressed or disappointed only weakens you further. It takes away your drive and makes you less effective.

On a positive note, there are two things you can almost always control — your mind and your body.

There's a reason men in prison exercise and read all the time. It's within their control. They broaden their minds and strengthen their bodies. They do this to stay sane in an environment they have no control over.

When I was young, I was unhappy with my home life. Some of it was justified, some was just teenage bullshit, but it was all very real to me at the time.

Instead of trying to control the things I could, I became self-destructive and lashed out. I gave up self-control, and by doing that, I stopped actively steering the direction of my life.

Those actions cost me time and had a negative impact on my future. I was lucky, it could've been worse. I eventually took charge of my life, joined the Army, and got back on track.

If you stop taking an active part in steering your future, you'll only end up somewhere good by sheer dumb luck, which is not likely. At best, taking a "whatever" attitude is a waste of time. At worst, it'll destroy your life.

You may find yourself feeling directionless or depressed, either now or sometime down the road. Step up and take control. Do what you can to improve your situation, even if it's just one small thing a day.

If you can't improve your situation, improve yourself; read, study and get fit. Strengthen your mind and body.

You aren't magically going to become a yoked, kick-ass, highly-skilled stud smothered in ladies. It doesn't work that way. You make it happen little-by-little, piece-by-piece. You slowly build yourself into who you want to be. It takes time and effort, but a strong mind and a strong body makes everything easier in life.

Opportunity will present itself at some point; maybe tomorrow, maybe a year from tomorrow. Be ready. Build yourself a strong mind and body, then seize opportunity when it does happen. This is how to maximize your chance at success and happiness.

Desire

Desire is a great motivator. Imagine how boring life would be if you didn't want anything?

Throughout history, desire has given a lot of people the drive to get off their ass.

First off, realize you'll always want. It's human nature. When you have a bike, you want a car. When you have a car, you want a nicer car. On and on it goes. When you get what you want, it won't end your wanting. You'll just move on to wanting something else.

Desire is good in the right amount; it can push you to make changes and it encourages self-improvement. As you progress towards your goals, you get a sense of satisfaction.

But if it's unrealistic, inappropriate or excessive, it can lead to frustration, depression and bad decision making.

If there's no way you're going to get the object of your desire, it's a waste of effort. Move on. I'm not saying don't shoot for the stars. I'm saying the odds of you sleeping with a movie star if you're 14 and live in Iowa are pretty slim.

You're much better off concentrating on something you can get.

Finally, understand temptation is often desire disguised as opportunity. Something you want becomes available, but at a price you know you shouldn't pay. A price you can't afford.

That price could be monetary; the object of your desire costs more money than you should spend.

The price could be criminal; you can have what you want, but you'll have to steal or hurt someone to get it.

The price could be social; you can sleep with someone's girlfriend, but if people find out you'll be hated.

This is extremely important when it comes to women, who are often considered man's greatest temptation.

Don't take advantage of girls. If you find yourself in a position of power, conduct yourself properly.

Don't betray your friends. Are you willing to sacrifice your friendships for the object of your desire? It may seem important at the time, but true friends will prove invaluable throughout your life.

If any goal becomes more important than the people in your life, you've got a problem you need to fix.

Don't convince yourself it's OK for this reason or that. That's mental and moral weakness trying to convince you to trade away your honor instead of putting in the work.

It's called temptation and not opportunity for a reason. You know you shouldn't do it, so don't.

Given all those warnings, how do you handle desire in a constructive way? First make sure your desire is realistic, appropriate and not excessive. Then, determine both where you are and where the goal is. If it's quite a distance, it's going to take some time. Break it down into small steps. Consider each of the important ones a milestone.

Focus on each milestone, but only one at a time. By doing that you make progress, which in turn keeps you motivated and happy.

If your milestones are too far apart, you'll feel overwhelmed and get bummed out. It'll seem like you're not getting anywhere.

If you can't reach a milestone, figure out why you're failing. Set a closer milestone, make some changes, then go back at it.

Don't get frustrated when you don't get what you want right away. All the good stuff takes both work and patience.

If it was quick or easy, everyone would have it. If everyone had it, you probably wouldn't want it in the first place. It's a weird circle, but that's often how it goes.

In a way, life is you wanting one thing after the next, and disappointment is inevitable. Don't let it break you, let it keep you hungry.

Hate

You are ultimately responsible for your actions and you're going to create trouble for yourself if you can't control your emotions.

Hate's one of the big two you need to get a handle on. Love's the other.

People often hate things that reflect their own personal shortcomings. Unpopular people hate popular people, poor people hate rich people, out of shape people hate models. This type of hate reflects the hater's own failure and shame.

Popular people may be popular because they're kind. Rich people may be rich because they work incredibly hard. Models may be in great shape because they spend hours in the gym every week.

Even if that isn't the case, even if in your opinion, they don't deserve what they have, it's pointless to hate them for it.

Jealous hate accomplishes nothing and poisons your resolve. It's just an excuse to side-step your own shortcomings.

After all, if you're realistic and face your failures head on, you'll realize fixing them is going to take a lot of work. It's far easier to avoid all the soul searching and just hate anyone who has it better than you — far easier, but wrong.

So, if you catch yourself hating someone, make sure you're not using hate to hide your own failure. You may find the problem isn't him, it's you.

Another thing to watch out for; if someone knows you hate something, he can use that knowledge to manipulate you. Once used, you're sacrificed. He'll get what he wants. You'll pay the price.

No moral person encourages hate in another. If someone is encouraging you to hate, realize he's sending you down a path of his choosing.

But let's say you do have a valid reason to hate someone. He's been cruel or hurt someone you care about. Embracing hatred is still not the winning play.

When you hate someone, it's easy to oversimplify things. You can become impulsive and make bad decisions that come back to hurt you, so don't surrender to it. Step back.

Hate's only value is motivation, and generally it's not worth the price. If you're hating something or someone, calm down and get some distance. Take the time to evaluate it properly and judge the truth with clear eyes.

Then, if you decide you must act, you can do it with a level head.

FIRST...THE BAD STUFF

Failure

You'll see failure in your life. People will fail you, even the ones you love.

Bad luck and timing play a part in failure, but generally people fail because they have a physical, mental or moral weakness.

If someone is failing but still trying, encourage him so he can grow stronger. But don't help too much. If you carry him, he'll never grow.

If he stops trying, make sure he recognizes his limits. Don't allow him to trick you into carrying him somewhere he doesn't belong.

If someone doesn't have the strength to get somewhere on his own, he doesn't have the strength to stay there. When he starts to slip, he'll grab you on his way down.

Other people's success or failure is generally out of your hands, so let us move on to something you can control — you.

You will fail — repeatedly.

You'll fail others and you'll fail yourself.

At some point, you'll fail to live up to some part, or a few sections, or maybe even most of the stuff in this book.

Don't accept it casually. It should hurt. But you must also understand: failure is part of growth. If you never fail, you're not pushing yourself.

If you keep trying and keep pushing, you'll do greater and greater things. Try until you fail, then try again — until you fail. Then try again.

If you try and never fail, you've set the bar too low. You're staying in your comfort zone, and if you make any progress, it'll be very slow.

Think of failure as the water between the stepping stones across the river to greatness. If you want to do great things, expect to get wet.

Shame

If you tell me you've managed to get through life so far without feeling shame, I'd call you a liar. That'd be the same as saying you've never failed.

Failure's best buddy is shame, which is you telling yourself you could've done better.

If you care about what you're trying to do and fail — shame. If you fail because you're weak — shame. It happens when you disappoint others and it lowers their opinion of you, and it's worse when you disappoint yourself.

If you stop feeling shame, one of two things have happened. You've either not disappointed yourself in a while or you've stopped being honest in your self-evaluation. The first is questionable: are you still pushing yourself? The second is unquestionably bad.

If you stop being honest when evaluating your own actions, you'll stop growing.

Always be honest with yourself. If you know you could've done better, recognize it and do better next time.

FIRST...THE BAD STUFF

Don't let shame eat you up or paralyze you. Remember everyone makes mistakes so learn from them. That's how you grow.

Self-Pity

Eventually you'll realize, if you haven't already, nothing in life is fair.

What you or your friends think you deserve doesn't amount to shit.

The quicker you get over this, the better you'll do. If you're waiting for what you deserve and what's fair to catch up to you, you'll be waiting forever.

Sometimes you'll get lucky and get what you think you deserve, but more often you won't.

This is because you don't determine what you deserve — chance, timing and other people do.

When people have what you want (money, recognition, a job, sex), they decide if they'll give it to you. They decide what you deserve. And remember, they're operating from a position of self-interest.

Why would they want to recognize what you deserve and then become obligated to give you something?

It makes more sense for them to not recognize it and keep what they have. It's human nature.

The same goes for work. Want a dollar? Do two dollars of work and you might get it. Do one dollar of work, expect to get fifty cents. Don't like it? Quit and then see how much money you get.

Once you get used to doing two dollars of work and getting paid a dollar, you'll discover the guy next to you, the one who's doing one dollar of work and getting paid fifty cents, is going to claim, "It's not fair!"

"Why are you getting a dollar and I'm only getting fifty cents!"

See how that works? He's not going to step outside himself and recognize you should be getting paid two dollars. He's going to focus on himself and how he's getting short changed. If you ever start down that road, recognize this in yourself.

It's easy to ignore your own shortcomings and blame others for your position in life. You'll never improve and end up constantly frustrated if you take this kind of attitude.

Does another kid at school have a great gaming system, better than yours? Maybe he has rich parents. Maybe he goes out and mows lawns. Maybe he deserves it, maybe he doesn't. You probably don't know the entirety of his situation, but either way, it's not your concern.

You need to focus on yourself and getting what you want. Don't worry about the other guy.

If you want something, you can make the decision to work for it, or just go ahead and keep wishing. If you work hard enough, you'll get it. If you only wish, it'll never happen.

There's an old saying "If wishes were horses, beggars would ride." This means despite all his wishes, the type of person who's unwilling to work (a beggar) will never have a horse. You must work to get what you want.

FIRST...THE BAD STUFF

It doesn't matter where you find yourself, self-pity does nothing. It doesn't make things better. It doesn't make you rich, get you a girlfriend or resurrect your dog.

Recognize self-pity, put it aside, move on. Otherwise it'll steal your motivation and provide resentment in return.

Don't soak up other people's sympathy, either. It may feel nice to get someone's pity but it too, is meaningless. They aren't doing you any favors by feeling sorry for you. They're sapping your will to get back up and try harder.

Most people just stumble through life, taking it as it comes. Few make a conscious decision to do the work, suffer the failures and make themselves into something.

One final thought on self-pity; understand every physical thing can be taken from you — all your possessions and everything you love.

What cannot be stolen is your past and who you are — your character. You can only give that away, destroying the best parts of yourself, piece-by-piece, through weakness and bad decision making.

FIRST...THE BAD STUFF

Your past is the sum of your actions up to this point. If you've put in the work, made good decisions and are proud of what you've done, you have a treasure no one can take.

FIRST...THE BAD STUFF

NOW...THE NORMAL STUFF

School

School is your first social training ground outside the home. Besides the obvious subjects of reading, writing and math, it's the primary place you learn to get along with other human beings.

In school, you explore the various social orders and try to figure out where you fit in. You discover the pecking order. Upperclassmen (juniors and seniors) are one group, lowerclassmen (freshmen and sophomores) another — separate groups based solely on grade. They're groups that have nothing to do with what anyone actually knows.

Some freshmen may know more than some seniors. Despite this, freshmen need to understand they're generally not welcome in the seniors group. They risk confrontation if they forget this.

This isn't to say it's impossible to become friends with people in a higher grade. It's to show, despite being physically or mentally equal, a division of groups exists.

This is how society works on a larger scale. It doesn't necessarily matter how smart or strong you are. You may be excluded from some groups based entirely on social factors.

Often these factors can be overcome, but they can't be ignored. If you ignore them, you'll fail and never understand why.

The various other social groups in school; emos, jocks, nerds and so on, all work the same. You need to understand the underlying social factors before you try to navigate them.

What do the members have in common? Are they the same age or do they share a common interest (music, sports, engineering etc.)? Did they all grow up together? Are their parents friends? These types of groups form naturally based on shared traits.

If you don't share this common trait or interest, the odds of you joining that group go down.

Then there's the teachers. Some will be professional and mature, but unfortunately, some won't be. Despite this, the social separation between student and teacher exists for a reason. It isn't naturally occurring, it's deliberately created to give the teachers control over the students. Society decided teachers need this authority to promote learning.

It's the teacher's responsibility to maintain this social order. If he loses it by not enforcing the written and unwritten rules of conduct, the line between teacher and student blurs. If he allows this line to blur, he loses the power the separation provides. Students stop taking him seriously.

Unfortunately, you're going to encounter incompetent people in positions of authority throughout life. School is just your first taste.

So, you may have a couple teachers you don't respect, and that's fine. Odds are they still know something you don't, plus they have the legitimate authority to make your life difficult. Those combine to make paying attention a good idea even if you don't actually respect them.

The stated purpose of school is to provide you with an education. It certainly does that. However, there are many forms.

There are the academic classes like reading, writing and arithmetic. Then there's social education, street smarts and common sense. In school, you get them all.

Learning how to deal with an authority figure you don't respect is a valuable social skill. If you can't, you're going to have problems later in life.

Make the most of your time in school. Ensure you learn and understand the academic curriculum. You may think you don't need to know these things, that you won't need them in your chosen career field or life in general. Every young person before you thought the same thing, and they all turned out wrong.

You don't know now what you'll need to know in the future, so learn all you can.

Fortunately, even the worst public school can give you the basics. As much as they may bore you, learn them or you'll run into issues as you grow older. People will judge you based on your knowledge. This can either create opportunities or close doors.

When you get frustrated, remind yourself you must be in class a set amount of time. It's not like you can leave, and you generally can't do something else, so make the best use of your time. Learn the lessons.

If you're mastering all your academic classes and you're still bored, spend time studying the other subjects. The stuff not on the official curriculum. Figure out how the groups work. Figure out how people work. Sharpen your social education. But don't be disruptive, unless you want some practice dealing with extra attention from an authority figure you probably don't respect.

NOW...THE NORMAL STUFF

Mom

For those of you with a mother in your life, there's a good chance you're reading this because dad's not around.

If so, you're not unique. Over the last forty years, this has become pretty common (I grew up that way myself). It doesn't create a sob story you can use to justify bad behavior. You're still responsible for your actions.

First off, understand not everyone is born with the same opportunities. Don't listen to anyone telling you otherwise. It's simply not true. People aren't born equal.

Some have wealthy parents and grow up in loving two-parent households. Others are born and immediately placed in foster care, never meeting their real parents.

The good news is, it's not the starting line that counts. It's the finish line. And all the opportunity in the world is no guarantee of success. Results only happen when you apply yourself to those opportunities you do get. If you don't apply yourself, don't expect results.

If you've had a rough start, you'll be tempted to blame your background for the troubles in your life. Before you do, make sure you've really made the most of every opportunity that came your way.

All that aside, assigning blame won't improve your results anyway. It only feeds your internal sympathy engine. You'll continue to do poorly, but probably at a faster pace.

History is full of men who came up in hard times and went on to become successful. It's also full of wealthy sons who managed to destroy their lives through weakness and bad decision making.

If you've got a great mom, or better yet, great parents, appreciate it. Like everyone, you'll still face challenges in life — things you may catch yourself calling unfair. But realize you've got it better than many, at least in the parent department.

There are plenty of moms with low paying jobs, not enough money for a house, and little time for their children. This may describe you.

If that's the case, maybe you live in a shitty apartment in a bad neighborhood. Maybe you live with another family, maybe you share a room.

Maybe your mom couldn't give you the best start. But if she bought you this book, she's clearly trying to make sure you end up a good man.

If you must judge your mom, look at the effort she's putting forth. Is she feeding you? Do you have a roof over your head? Are you living in a safe environment? That's about all she's required to provide.

If she spends time with you, does things you're interested in or tries to make you happy, she certainly cares about you.

Look. Your mom is just a person, and 15 to 20 years ago she was just as inexperienced as you are now. Imagine that.

Hopefully, you've figured out you don't have all the answers. You don't have the life experience to know how all the games are played. At your age, she didn't either and maybe she still doesn't.

There's a good chance either your mom wasn't married, or she got divorced soon after having you. She probably raised you on her own. Maybe her family helped, maybe not. That's a tough situation either way, so don't make things more difficult than they already are. Don't act up and create problems.

When you make things difficult for your mom, it eventually snaps back and bites you in the ass.

She only has so much time and money, and if you make her spend it getting you out of trouble, she won't have anything left for the good stuff.

Keep it up and she'll eventually get tired of your bullshit. You won't like the result.

Now, you may be thinking "But what about her bullshit?" I understand your mom could be doing things that frustrate you.

If she thinks there's no male role model in your life, she might be pushing you to do manly things; forcing you to play sports, take martial arts or join the Scouts. Hopefully you enjoy these activities, but maybe because you feel pressured, you don't.

Your mom could also have wanted a girl. She could be reliving her childhood through you, or simply not understand boys and girls are interested in different activities. She's forcing you to do stuff you have zero interest in; like dance, singing or theater.

Try to take it in stride and get something out of it, even if you're not interested.

As a man there are times you have to spend, and things you have to do for others, regardless of whether you enjoy it or not. The sooner you get used to this, the less frustrating it'll be.

If these activities become unbearable, have a discussion with her. A reasonable discussion, not a fight. Think about what you are going to say and why — before you say it.

On the other hand, your mom could be ignoring you. Maybe she feels you're old enough now she doesn't have to spend time with you. Maybe she's trying to recover the youth she traded to be a mother; partying, staying out late, or bringing home strangers — not thinking about how that impacts you.

I'm telling you all this to help you understand her, not to judge your mom a good or a bad person. It doesn't particularly matter. What matters is what you make of yourself, because of, or in spite of, your environment.

What goes on in your head is the most important factor in what kind of man you become. Not your environment, but how you react to it. Not how many opportunities you get, but what you make of them.

No matter how bad your starting situation is, it's where you end up that matters. You've got between here and there to make it happen. You.

Dad

Prior to the 1980s, most fathers had the opportunity to teach their sons; giving them a jump start on manhood and life's hard lessons.

I'm sure you've realized this is no longer true. Many boys are raised with little or no involvement from dad.

It's now common to see dad only on the weekends or during the summer. Maybe he's in prison. Maybe he's a single guy living alone somewhere. Maybe he has a new wife and now he's dad to some kids you've never met.

If he was ever around to begin with, dad could be absent now for a number of reasons.

If you do have a father in your life, with any luck, he's a good guy. If so, I would expect he's teaching you the things in this book. If that's the case, the book should serve to fill in some gaps and support his points. (If what you read sounds like what your dad's telling you, maybe he isn't crazy after all.)

No matter what your current parent situation is, things can always change. There might be more marriages, divorces or unexpected roommates. After all, you can't control your parents.

What you can control is you — how you look at life, and how you play the cards you've been dealt.

Don't let any chaos going on at home overwhelm you. You probably can't avoid it entirely, but don't dive into it. Fixing it isn't your responsibility. If you get overly involved, you'll frustrate yourself and you could actually make things worse.

Your parents will make mistakes, they all do. Often the mistakes only create minor problems, but sometimes they create catastrophes.

All you can do is learn from both their good and bad decisions. You're neither doomed to repeat them, nor are you guaranteed to inherit them.

Make decisions about what you want in life, then act. Make your life a good one.

Family

Family: the friends you don't get to choose.

Family should be viewed as either associates you must spend time around, or friends (unless they're acting as your parents, in which case, you should treat them as such). Observe how they behave, both toward you and others, then treat them accordingly.

For some reason there's a popular myth family always has your best interest at heart. "Blood is thicker than water" is an old saying people often repeat. It means you can count on your family more than other people. Sadly, this is not always the case.

Character counts far more than being related. Hopefully your family is full of people with character. Unfortunately, it's probably a mix of all sorts.

Likely some members of your family will be good, some bad, some generous and some greedy. Some of them you may trust with your life, and I'd bet a few can't be trusted at all.

So let their actions be your guide. You get to decide what kind of relationship you have beyond being polite at family functions.

People

In life, you're going to meet all sorts of people. Unfortunately, many will be self-serving and weak.

Our society has stopped demanding character of people. First world countries have gotten so wealthy, we can now afford weakness.

Technology has advanced to the point we produce excess resources. Automation also allows us to produce resources with far less human involvement. As a result, we have a growing population of idle people who don't produce anything, they only consume.

So long as things don't get too far out of balance, these non-producers aren't a direct threat. There is, however, unseen damage — weakness has grown in the absence of challenge.

Historically, just surviving long enough to raise children was a challenge in itself. Hunger, disease and primitive medicine tested people. Surviving required strength, character and often luck.

That is no longer the case. Now, we have social programs that provide food, housing and medical care. No effort is required other than signing up and jumping through some paperwork hoops.

All these programs were designed to help people, and often they do work. However, they have the unintended consequence of removing the challenges that made people strong.

People who have never overcome challenges are weaker than those who have. But who wants to face a difficult truth? It's easier to convince themselves they're someone they're not, which creates another problem. They don't know their own limitations.

Almost everyone tells themselves they're good and strong. The reality is many people are neither good nor strong and can't be trusted any further than their own self-interest.

Despite this, even the people fooling themselves still recognize real strength. When they see it, they are either drawn to it or repulsed by it.

They're drawn to it if it can protect them or if they want to become strong themselves, it's an example they can look up to.

Strength repulses people who know there's no chance they'll become greater than they are now. They don't want to see what they cannot be.

Be wary of these poisonous people. They dislike the very existence of strength. They sabotage efforts and try to bring others down to their level. They criticize the strong and try to turn others against them.

If you find yourself involved with people like this, keep your distance. Find a new job if you can't avoid them at work or find a new house if they're your roommates. Do what it takes to get them out of your life. Make new friends.

Poisonous people drag you down whenever they get a chance. Everything becomes more difficult, and life is hard enough. If you can't avoid them, recognize what they're doing and work around it. Let them inspire you to double your efforts. Once you work past them, you'll be stronger for having overcome their resistance.

Try to remember most people aren't doing things for your benefit. They're doing them out of self-interest.

Luckily, in most cases the interests of those around you generally align with your own, so there's nothing wrong with it. Just be aware.

When it comes to people in general, don't share your thoughts or feelings with people who won't value them. You're setting yourself up for disappointment.

Likewise, don't assume someone you know casually is interested in what you have to say. It may be boring or make no sense to him without context.

When you overshare, you're also teaching that person how you think and what your motivations are. If he's weak or selfish, he can use that information to manipulate you.

People of character; strong and good people, will seldom try to disguise their motivation. Weak people often will. They'll tell you they're doing things in your interest to reduce your resistance to something that only benefits them. Pay attention. Over time you'll learn to recognize these people.

The only time good people hide their motivation is when it's actually in your best interest, but they wouldn't have your consent. In these cases, you generally won't know until after the fact anyway.

On occasion, take a few minutes and look back. You may find treasure you might otherwise miss, like the person who did things behind the scenes and never sought your recognition.

Sometimes the best people don't draw attention to themselves. Either their kindness was exploited in the past or they don't want people's gratitude to create an obligation.

Given you'll be dealing with people almost every day for the rest of your life, here's the best advice I can give: judge people by what they do, not what they say. Observe how they treat others. This will prove useful in sorting out the good from the bad.

NOW...THE NORMAL STUFF

Associates

The humans you deal with regularly who aren't close enough to be actual friends, and not far enough to be just people, are your associates.

This group includes the bulk of folks you know. They're OK. You can have some laughs with them, socialize and enjoy their company.

However, you need to distinguish between associates and friends. There's a big difference.

Friends will do things for you, even if it costs them time, money or effort.

Generally, an associate will only do things if it's cost-free. He may lend you a hammer, but he won't help you build a fence. That's fine. So, don't ask an associate for help with anything significant, you'll only end up disappointed.

What if someone you knew but didn't really consider a friend, asked you to come over and help him with something that might take hours? You might do it, but if you did you'd feel put out. If later you asked him to return the favor and he refused, you'd be disappointed.

On anything big you only ask your friends. People who ask associates for help are often considered users. If you ask an associate he may think "Oh we must be friends, I hadn't realized but OK I'll help." Later if he asks you, assuming you're friends and you say no, he'll think you used him earlier by pretending to be friends.

In life, almost everyone you know will be an associate.

Treat them as you'd expect them to treat you. Don't take advantage of them. Don't allow them to take advantage of you.

Language

How you talk among your friends is one thing, how you talk in mixed company is another. Mind your tongue.

It may seem trivial and unimportant, but people notice how you speak and they'll judge you by it.

When you think of someone who sounds dumb what does he sound like? Does he have an accent, a southern drawl or speak a certain way? Does he use a certain type of slang?

When you think of someone respectable what does he sound like? How about a criminal?

How you speak will be one of many things people use in their effort to figure you out.

Although there's scientific evidence to the contrary, profanity and vulgarity are viewed as unintelligent and crude. When you curse and swear all the time, people think you're uneducated and rude.

The same goes for slang. Don't speak informally or use slang with people outside your group of friends.

When you're with a group of peers or near equals take your guidance from the leader. If he's cussing and using profanity, it's probably OK for you to do the same.

Different groups of people have different expectations on acceptable language. If you want to be accepted and respected by the group, keep your language within those boundaries.

Appearance

Work on your appearance. Despite what some people claim, you're constantly judged on appearance.

First off, come to terms with the fact there are always some things beyond your control. If you're going through puberty, you may be much taller or shorter than others in your class. You might be skinny or have bad acne.

While these things may seem incredibly important now, put them in perspective. Maybe your body is still growing. If so, that'll finish soon. Most of these issues will resolve themselves on their own so don't get hung up on them. But some of them won't.

Remember the part about not everyone being born equal? Throughout life there are always going to be people taller, faster or better looking than you.

The good news is girls are generally not as interested in a boy's appearance as you might think. Unlike boys, girls are likely to find you attractive if you're funny, confident and demonstrate good character.

This becomes even more important as you get older and the girls become women. The most attractive boy doesn't always get the most attractive girl.

Enough about the things you can't control, let's discuss the things you can; fitness, cleanliness and clothes.

Understand if you're overweight most people assume you have little self-control. They think you eat too much and don't exercise. They may never say it, they may deny even thinking it, but it's always there in the back of their minds.

Unless you have some rare genetic disorder, they're right. Don't fool yourself. You can't get fat unless you eat too much, and too much varies by the person. Some people can eat whatever they want and not get fat, some people tend to store every extra calorie around their waist. That being said, watch what and how much you eat.

If you're overweight, other overweight people will tell you it's OK, and not your fault. They tell you this because if they admit it's a lack of self-control, they have to point the finger back at themselves.

You'll find weak people make excuses for your failures the same way they excuse their own. On the surface they do it to appear kind and sympathetic. But in many cases, it's only so they can feel free to use the same excuse. Don't accept that and don't do it.

Be honest with yourself if you want to improve. If you're going to bullshit yourself, you're going nowhere.

This isn't to say you should go around shaming fat people. Being fat is their issue, not yours. Most certainly don't say anything just to be hurtful. Fat people know they're fat. There's no need to point it out. You don't have to agree with the excuses, just be polite. It's none of your business, anyway. You have enough to worry about.

Exercise and stay active so you don't become overweight. If you're fat now, own it and make the decision to do something about it. Take control of yourself.

Cleanliness is also part of appearance. Bathe regularly and use deodorant. Brush your teeth, floss and trim your finger and toenails. If you're going to use cologne, don't overdo it. Simple stuff, but it matters.

The last part of this section; your haircut, visible tattoos, piercings and clothes.

While you're a young person, society will be more accepting of a nontraditional appearance — more accepting, not entirely accepting. You'll likely just experience fewer negative consequences than you would as an adult.

Regardless of your character, most people judge you primarily based on your appearance and how you talk. They seldom get an opportunity to find out who you really are.

If you're OK with that, go ahead and dress however you'd like. But don't get upset later they didn't give you a fair evaluation.

With your haircut and clothes, you're telling people "This is how I choose to present myself." Even if you don't realize it, you're making a statement.

You may be some intriguing, multi-faceted puzzle. But people generally don't have time to play the "who is this person actually deep down inside?" game. It's self-centered to assume anyone owes you the time and effort required to figure out who you really are.

If you choose to ignore this advice, don't be outraged when people judge you based on how you look, talk and act. People make snap, sometimes unconscious, judgments based on your appearance and behavior.

They drop you into a category and move on. Their behavior towards you will be based on the category they've assigned. Give that some thought. You don't want to be in a category they don't respect if you need them to cooperate with you at some point in the future.

NOW...THE NORMAL STUFF

Judging

For some reason, not being judgmental is considered a virtue these days. I don't know where that came from, but it's garbage.

Anyone who claims to not be judgmental is either fooling himself or attempting to fool you.

Judgment is the basis of reason. If you walk around not judging you'll end up continually surprised, frequently exploited and generally disappointed.

People will often take advantage of you or just fail you over and over. In a worst-case scenario, you could end up victimized or killed if you fail to properly judge someone as a threat.

You need to judge all the time. You judge others, they judge you. Now your initial judgments won't always be correct, so don't jump right to your final conclusion. But that first impression gives you a starting position.

If you have the time, desire or necessity, you can continue to watch and evaluate. Your opinion may change based on what you see.

Understand, you'll be judged too. If you adopt the clothing, style and slang of a criminal subculture, guess what? Everyone's going to assume you're a criminal. Surprise! Expect extra attention from police and store security.

Among the things you'll be judged on: how you talk, how you carry yourself, the things you do and fail to do, the clothes you wear, your haircut, piercings and tattoos, the music you listen to and the car you drive. The list goes on and on.

People gather all these facts to create a snapshot of you based on the information immediately available. You should do the same.

When you see someone on the street, you have no idea if he's kind-hearted and volunteers at an animal rescue, or in the habit of stealing anything not bolted down.

Most of the time, you won't have the opportunity to figure out if there's more to someone than it appears. You take the information you have available, which is often only appearance, and go from there.

NOW...THE NORMAL STUFF

A final word of caution, there are many people who know how to play the appearance game.

You may have heard the term "A wolf in sheep's clothing." The worst human monsters know how important appearances can be and use that against their victims by dressing and speaking in a nonthreatening manner.

These people will deliberately look like something they're not, just to get your guard down.

So, don't allow yourself to get into a vulnerable position around anyone until you've seen how he conducts himself.

If you're going to protect yourself and the people you care about, you need to be aware of your surroundings. Ultimately, people are almost always the greatest threat.

Don't trust anyone you don't know well, even if you get a positive first impression. Exercise good judgement.

NOW...THE NORMAL STUFF

Sports and Fitness

Play sports if possible, it's great mental, physical and social training. You'll improve your fitness and learn the value of determination, competitiveness and cooperation. Being fit makes you happier and healthier. You'll live longer, feel better and look better doing it.

As I've repeatedly mentioned, that people judge you based on appearance and fitness is very apparent.

Females judge you and that impacts your ability to get a quality girlfriend.

Males judge you too, perhaps more than women. They see you as either a rival, a weakness or an asset to the tribe. Men are subconsciously tribal, and the strong ones seldom invite weak males into their tribe.

Physically, people who appear strong and healthy are given more opportunities than those who appear unhealthy or overweight. They get better job offers, have fuller social lives and generally make more money. People want to be around them.

NOW...THE NORMAL STUFF

One minor side note when it comes to fitness, if you get extremely muscular some people may conclude your entire life revolves around the gym. While this may not be true at all, they may judge you as unintelligent or one-dimensional.

Don't let me worry you though, getting extremely muscular takes years of hard work. You won't wake up one day and find you've overdone it. So if you're passionate about it, become a powerlifter or bodybuilder. Just recognize you may face some prejudices.

If you don't like sports, or find you're not very good at them, you still have an obligation to maintain a certain level of fitness. When you're healthy and strong you're an asset, if you're sickly and weak, a liability.

The benefits of physical training, whether in individual and group sports or general strength and conditioning cannot be emphasized enough.

You want to be fit.

Games

There's nothing wrong with playing video games, but don't let it take over your life.

You have obligations. As a young guy, these probably include school and cleaning up after yourself. If you're old enough, hopefully you have a job and a girlfriend as well. These things come before video games.

In addition to your obligations, you also need social skills. In life you'll constantly need to talk to people you don't know. You want to do this well. It's a real skill you can improve, and it matters.

You sharpen your social skills by talking to strangers out in the real world. By the way, the whole "don't talk to strangers" thing is for children. The rule ends when your balls drop. By now you should be able to judge who you should and who you shouldn't talk to.

It's easy to talk to your friends. If you play games online, you're used to talking to other players. You might be great at teasing, trolling or talking shit. That's not the kind of talking I'm talking about.

Remember women and girls? You need to learn how to socialize with girls in a way that doesn't weird them out. Some of them won't be comfortable if you talk to them the same way you talk online.

Policemen, doctors, teachers, judges, your boss: They're all different types of people. They expect to be spoken to in certain ways. The kind of practice you need to talk to these folks, you won't get playing video games.

You generally can't joke around with policemen. If you do, they'll probably get pissed. That can cause you plenty of grief.

If you're in a courtroom and you speak improperly to a judge, you can end up in jail. If you're rude, yell, curse or talk when it isn't your turn, you can be charged with contempt of court. It's a real crime and you can end up behind bars, whether you think it's fair or not.

NOW...THE NORMAL STUFF

Getting and keeping a job requires social skills as well, and the better your social skills are, the more successful you'll be. You may not think it matters, but it most certainly does.

What this all comes down to is don't nerd out so hard on games you fail to meet your obligations, or your social skills suffer. Remember, playing games is a leisure activity. Never let it come before your obligations or personal development.

The order is; things you must do such as work; things you should do like exercise; then finally, things you can do — if you have any time left. Gaming is in the last category.

NOW...THE NORMAL STUFF

Work

Nothing prepares you for life like your first couple jobs. Get a job as soon as you're able.

If you're too young to work outside the home, see if your mother or a relative will pay you to complete a task.

Make a deal to do something in exchange for money, then do it. But don't half-ass it and expect to get paid. That's not how the world works.

People don't give their money away. If they're paying you, they expect value.

If your first paying job is from a family member, and you don't do the work properly, I sincerely hope he doesn't pay you. He's setting you up to fail in life if he does. Out in the real world, half-ass work gets you fired.

Don't get used to people giving you things and don't take anything you didn't earn. Taking things you didn't earn weakens you. It also creates an obligation to the person who gave it to you.

If someone gives you something you didn't work for, he's going to expect something in return. Down the road, he may remind you; you owe him.

Sometimes this isn't a big deal, he may only want help moving or fixing something. But sometimes it is. He may ask you to do something you don't want to do, or something you know you shouldn't. Don't allow yourself to be put in that position.

That aside, obviously don't take on so much work your schooling suffers but do get a start in the workplace.

Let me warn you, the people you meet at work won't all be great. You'll meet some real turds, but you'll meet turds throughout your life. The sooner you get practice spotting and avoiding them, the better. As you can imagine, you want to keep your interaction with turds to a minimum.

Once you start seeing the results of consistent work — money, respect and pride in a job well done, you'll begin to appreciate your own efforts.

Procrastination

Remember the section on Failure? You can also fail through procrastination, which is just another word for laziness.

You put something off by telling yourself you'll get to it later. Later rolls around and you come up with another excuse.

Soon you have a bunch of tasks you're avoiding. All those tasks start to pile up and bum you out. They build up until they're overwhelming, and then serve as an added excuse to avoid something else.

"Well, I know I have to clean my room, but I have to take out the trash, too. Trash is more important, so I'd better do that first. Man ... I don't want to take out the trash right now. I'll take it out later tonight."

You've just prevented yourself from taking out the trash and cleaning your room, all in one excuse!

The funny thing is, you often spend more time coming up with excuses why you haven't done something than you would've spent doing it. We've all done this. No one is immune.

If you catch yourself trying to come up with an excuse to put something off, stop that thought before you finish.

If you know you have to take out the trash, so you start telling yourself, "Ugh trash, you know, I think I'm gonna take out the trash after...," just stop right there and take out the trash.

Practice this technique with all the little things. The minute you catch yourself thinking up an excuse, stop. Just do whatever it is you were going to talk yourself out of. Stop thinking and do it.

If you do this a few times, you'll see it works. Once you realize it works, it becomes easier to do. Ultimately, you'll save a lot of time and make yourself happier.

Things become more and more difficult the longer you let them sit. Trouble grows over time like a weed. If you pull it when it's small, it pops right out. If you let it grow and grow, when you finally go to pull it, it takes ten times the effort. And sometimes things can grow so big, when you do finally try to tackle it, it's too late. The damage is done and you can't fix it.

No one appreciates laziness and it'll hurt your relationships, both work and personal.

If people are counting on you and you don't get things done because you're lazy, it's considered weak and selfish. It can cost you jobs, friends and girlfriends.

Training yourself to not procrastinate takes effort. But it'll save you time and headaches in the long run. If you know something needs to be done, stop thinking about it and get to it.

NOW...THE NORMAL STUFF

Money

In modern society, the main result of work is money.

Money is neither good nor evil. How you get it, or what you do with it, maybe. But not money itself.

Money is the primary physical resource.

With money you can buy all the physical things you'll need in life; food, clothing and shelter. It can provide protection from the elements and protection from physical danger.

The more money your tribe has, the more successful it'll be. Money allows your tribe to grow.

With enough money, you can afford to raise children in a safe environment, one that gives them the greatest chance of growing up healthy and successful.

It's important to learn not only how to make money, but to budget and manage it as well. Most everyone understands the first part, but quite a few don't bother learning the second.

You can have a great job and bring home stacks of cash, but if you can't budget — if you spend too much — you're still broke. If you're always broke, you're always stressed.

Times have changed, and now the odds of the government or a private company supporting your retirement are slim. So you need to plan for your retirement now. It may sound ridiculous, but I'm not kidding. As soon as possible start budgeting, saving and investing.

If you can invest even a little and leave it alone, you'll thank yourself later. Compound interest on your savings means your money actually makes you more money over time. You don't have to do anything else, just leave it alone.

When you get a job and your employer offers a 401(k) plan, take it. Basically, you get paid more just for participating. Don't ignore this benefit. Also, it's worth repeating: no matter how tempting, don't touch your 401(k) money until you're ready to retire.

I know this is incredibly boring, but you need to understand money and how to budget, save and invest. Look up the terms online and start educating yourself.

Women want men who can provide for children. It sounds heartless, but it makes perfect sense.

Why would a successful woman have children with a poor man?

If she has money, she'll judge him. He doesn't have the skills and foresight to save and plan. This makes him risky as a potential father. He's not her equal, let alone a provider.

Generally, women don't "marry down," or choose someone less successful than themselves. This means if you're poor, the best you can expect is an equal. But it's likely you'll end up with someone even poorer.

Even if you have no intention of getting married, money still makes the world go around. Learn how to make it. Learn how to keep it.

One last thing on money. In life, despite your best efforts, you'll probably have high times and low times. Money will come and go.

As important and useful as money is, never compromise your integrity to get it. You can run out of self-respect, and unfortunately once it's gone, you can't run from it. If you compromise your integrity, for money or any other reason, you'll end up hating yourself.

FINALLY...THE GOOD STUFF

Heroes

What kind of man will you choose to become — or will you choose at all?

You have two paths ahead:

You can make no effort to steer your life, and just let it take you wherever.

Or

You can make a deliberate choice, and work to become the man you want to be.

Say you take the first path, and just let life take you wherever.

If you're lucky and happen to make the right decision at every fork in the road, you may end up respectable.

As an old man, you might be able to look back with pride.

You might, but it's unlikely.

Imagine trying to build something you've never built before, but you have no real skills. Maybe you've seen it once or twice. But you've never studied it, never taken it apart to see how it's put together.

The odds you'll randomly end up a man if you don't try, fail and try again, are about the same as you building a house the first time you pick up a hammer.

You need to spend time over the next few years and decide who you want to become. It's a lifetime pursuit but stick with the next few years for now. The most important years of your life.

The path you start on now is critical. "Well begun is half done," if you get a good start now, it's much easier to get a good finish.

If you choose to become a man, accept the fact it's going to take work. Start preparing yourself for success. As useful as this book may be, I can't cover everything. You need to find some role models.

Look carefully at the males around you. Decide if you want to be like them. Be certain they have the traits and behaviors you admire. If you find men worth following, show them respect. Learn what they're willing to teach.

If there are no worthy men in your life, you still have options.

Heroes have been deliberately created for you.

Heroes reflect the key virtues of manhood; strength, determination, courage and sacrifice. These qualities are hardwired into male genetic memory.

It's no mistake heroes are all similar in many ways. History records them and authors create them as the ultimate examples. Heroes are there for young men to follow when there's no one real to lead.

You don't have to pick just one hero either. You can pick and choose a combination with all the traits you admire.

Read and learn about them, study their successes and failures. Take the best qualities from each hero and put them together into the man you want to become.

Now you have the man in your life you can follow. Even if he isn't real, you are.

FINALLY...THE GOOD STUFF

Mentors

Consider mentors mini real-life-heroes. They might not have a hero's abilities, but they know something you need to learn and they're willing to teach you.

A mentor can have a huge impact on your life by teaching and providing opportunities you'd never get otherwise.

Being mentored is more of a circumstance than a definable thing. It's seldom officially recognized. No one in your life is going to come up one day and say "I'm going to mentor you. I am your mentor." (If someone does, you should be skeptical before you accept his assistance. That would be super weird.)

Often, you won't realize someone's been mentoring you until after the fact. You'll just suddenly recognize he helped and taught you, for no personal gain.

When you think about it, a mentor is willingly getting into an unfair trade with you. He's giving you something —

generally knowledge or opportunity — and expects nothing in return. He just wants to see you succeed.

If someone chooses to mentor you, it shows he cares about you. No other reason. It's a selfless act on his part. Your part of the bargain? Be respectful and pay attention.

Ignoring people's advice will often close doors just as they start to open. If someone considers mentoring you, then notices you ignoring people's suggestions, he won't bother. No one's going to waste time trying to teach someone who won't learn.

So, be an attentive and respectful student when someone's willing to teach. You never know who is watching.

Having a mentor is a significant opportunity. He'll often help you get jobs and introduce you to people you'd never meet on your own.

They only come along a few times in life, so if you disregard a chance, you may not get another.

Friends

As the saying goes, "Choose your friends wisely." Nothing has a greater impact on your life than the people you surround yourself with.

You can't pick your family, but you do get to choose your friends. So pick good, solid people you can trust.

Friends add value to your life, and you add value to theirs. This value should include entertainment, laughter, good advice and trust.

You must both add relatively equal value. If it seems he's adding far more than you, he may be a mentor and not a normal friend.

By the same token, don't pick friends you must constantly help. Some people always need saving and you'll get burned and bummed out trying.

Learn this quickly: everyone makes mistakes on occasion, but don't hang out with people who make them constantly.

FINALLY...THE GOOD STUFF

People like that aren't your friends, they are dependents. They can be your followers, underlings or associates, but never consider them friends.

Keep this in your mind: you get the kind of friendship you give. Strong people are discerning, and like attracts like. This means if you're a half-assed friend, unwilling to help on the rare occasion it's needed, you'll end up with similar friends.

In a friendship, you establish and accept limits. If you want a friend who'll always be there for you, you need to do the same in return.

Don't abuse your friends. Just because your friend is always willing, doesn't mean you should always call. Be considerate and expect similar consideration. Your friends are not your servants any more than you are theirs.

If you're the child of a single parent, you probably have more free time than someone with two full time parents. All this free time may bore you and lead you to spend more time with friends. In this case, it's even more important to have the right ones.

If you end up hanging out with people who are constantly in trouble, guess what? You'll soon join them. Doors to your future will start to close. If you get arrested and get a record, many doors slam shut.

Don't go out looking for trouble, and don't pick friends who do. Use the time with your friends constructively as opposed to destructively.

You can and should have adventures with your friends, but don't cross the line. Stay out of jail. All of you.

FINALLY...THE GOOD STUFF

Girls

Girls want boys. Females want males. Women want men.

Girls often want the bad boy, the tough guy, the rebel. These stereotypes all exhibit some of the traits of manhood. They might be physically strong, confident or willing to fight. That's what makes them appealing.

However, women want men — someone with all the traits of manhood — not just some.

Men are primarily protectors and providers. It makes sense when you think about it. Every living being's unconscious, biological goal is to have children. Women are drawn to men because they exhibit the traits most likely to ensure the survival of their children.

This preference has evolved over more than a hundred thousand years. It's a genetic hard-code that's difficult to ignore (though lately some people seem to be trying). It's there for good reason.

Food, shelter and medicine are far easier to get now than any time in the past. This might lead people to believe the built-in code is unnecessary. But there's no guarantee it will always be so.

Civilization has cycles of highs and lows.

While we're now primarily a nation of weak, fat bodies, there's no saying that kind of lifestyle will survive in the future. People understand this instinctively, so they're still drawn to people who express the gender ideals.

Following all the tenets of manhood as outlined in this book is difficult and often unrewarding. However, this is one place it does pay off.

It makes sense as a boy that you'll be with girls. But get far enough along on the path to manhood and you'll begin to attract women.

They're hard to find — as rare as men anymore.

But a woman is what you want, and they can be far more discerning.

Don't expect to attract a physically fit woman if you're an overweight slob, an accomplished woman if you're lazy, or a woman with character if you're a coward and a liar. It won't happen. Why would she be satisfied with that guy?

While a female may settle for almost any male if he has enough money (he's a provider at least), a woman doesn't need to.

She's earned a man. Be worthy.

FINALLY...THE GOOD STUFF

Confidence

Men are confident without being arrogant.

Confidence is measuring against yourself. You've compared yourself against the task and believe you measure up.

Arrogance is measuring against others. You've compared others against the task and believe you're their superior.

If a subject comes up, and you know you can do it, there's nothing wrong with saying so as long as you don't exaggerate.

There's also nothing wrong with believing yourself to be superior at a certain task, when compared to a specific person. Realistically, that may be the case. Maybe you and your friends agree you're a better baseball player than the kid in Apt. C.

The problems start when you broaden your comparison, like when you start to include groups of tasks or groups of people. The problem is fully revealed when you start telling people. Now you're just bragging.

Bragging and arrogance are not quite the same, but they're closely related.

Not all arrogant people brag. Sometimes, without saying a word, their attitude is enough to spot them.

Not all braggarts are arrogant. Many have the opposite problem of low self-esteem. These folks brag hoping it will make people like them.

True confidence is a people magnet. A confident person who isn't cocky, is likely to have more friends, of a better quality, than someone who's arrogant, uncertain or a braggart.

A braggart attracts people as well. After all, he wouldn't brag if it didn't work. But he only draws people who are gullible or have low self-esteem.

Consequently, because braggarts and bullshitters break two rules of manhood (**You will be honest with the tribe** and **You will do what you say**), they don't have quality friends. Exaggerating or outright lying makes planning impossible. You can't count on a bullshitter.

The kind of people you want to be around, are the kind who can spot and avoid a bullshitting loudmouth. Good people see it a mile away and keep their distance.

Ultimately, the only person who needs convincing is you. If you believe it, it shows as an easy confidence. You don't need to compare yourself to others, when you're satisfied with your measurement against yourself.

You'll come to realize the more a person talks about how good he is, the more likely he's pretending to be someone he wants to be, not someone he is.

You may have heard the terms "talk is cheap," "actions speak louder than words" or better yet, "deeds, not words." These all mean the same thing: don't go around telling people what you can do. When the time comes, show them.

FINALLY...THE GOOD STUFF

Humility

Confidence and humility are the opposite sides of a good coin. Arrogance and bragging are the opposite sides of a separate coin — entirely bad.

No matter how good you are, two things are true: you could be better, and there's someone better than you.

Humility serves a purpose: it keeps you improving.

If you believe you're the best, you stop pushing yourself. So, no matter how good you are (or think you are), recognize you could be better.

Don't just pretend to be humble in an effort to appear modest. Good people won't be fooled. Besides, pretending is external, it's about the audience. The lesson of humility is internal, it's about you. Stay honest in your self-evaluation and stay motivated to improve.

The word humility means being humble. If you don't choose that word for yourself, there's another word: humiliated. That's when life comes along and chooses it for you.

FINALLY...THE GOOD STUFF

FINALLY...THE GOOD STUFF

Self-Focus

Two things to understand:

1. You should demand more of yourself than you demand of others.
2. Everyone's primary responsibility is to themselves, but not at another's expense.

Those two things make up the difference between self-focused and selfish.

In most cases, the military pushes people harder than they've ever pushed themselves before. But by design, even the military has limits.

If someone is constantly raising expectations and holding you accountable, he can help you grow physical and moral strength. But if he does all the pushing, he takes away the critical resistance you need to overcome — your own mind.

To build mental strength, you need to overcome the resistance within that keeps you weak. Overcoming this builds will. Willpower is mental strength.

FINALLY…THE GOOD STUFF

Elite military unit's selection process tests for this. They'll let you quit. In fact, they encourage it. They're not just testing your physical strength. If you don't have the mental strength to stick it out, they don't want you. You'll fail when the going gets tough.

The best way to build mental strength is to first demand more from yourself and then hold yourself accountable.

It's impossible to build mental strength without pushing yourself, and because it's you challenging you, if you fail, you're entirely responsible. There's no one else to blame. You must come to terms with your own success or failure. No finger pointing, no excuses.

Obviously, your life shouldn't just revolve around tackling one personal challenge after the next. Life is empty if you're entirely self-focused.

You have plenty of living to do along the way and you'll cross paths with many people. And while this journey is yours, sometimes the moment is theirs. Recognize these moments. Put your needs aside and help, but don't allow anyone to take you off your path.

If you walk someone else's path, you never get to your destination. If you carry him to yours, he'll never reach his own.

Besides, many people stop walking if you're willing to carry them. Carry them long enough and they become your responsibility. They become so weak they can't walk on their own if you put them down.

In a circle of everyone helping the person in front of them and counting on being helped by the person behind, no one improves. If everyone grows weak by relying on others, no one has real strength when it's truly needed.

So, challenge and hold yourself accountable. And unless you want to weaken them, don't carry the people you care about.

FINALLY...THE GOOD STUFF

Protection

No, this section is not about condoms, though that brings up a good point: use them.

I'm talking about a man's obligation to protect himself and the people he cares about.

Most of the time this comes down to good decision making — staying out of dangerous situations and away from unpredictable people. After all, it's better to avoid danger than overcome it.

If you suddenly realize you're in a dangerous situation, get the people you care about out as quickly as possible.

As I've mentioned, if you are attacked, knowing how to defend yourself and loved ones is vital. But even more important is being smart enough to entirely avoid dangerous situations in the first place.

Unless you're a soldier, don't knowingly put yourself into situations where you'll need to fight, and don't make fighting your first response.

You'll create unnecessary trouble for yourself and the very people you're trying to protect.

Finally, there's more to protection than just safety from danger.

Making good decisions in life, earning decent money and being mentally and morally strong allows you to protect people in other, not so apparent, ways.

You can provide housing, food and an education.

You can teach people and prepare them for life's difficulties, helping them become strong enough to protect themselves when you're not around.

Emotion

Emotions are perfectly healthy.

Get angry at exploitation and cruelty. Love the good people in your life. Be sad when you lose something you care for.

The advice in this handbook may leave you with the impression that to be a man is to be cold and unfeeling. That's not the intent.

It comes down to this: you either control your emotions or let them control you.

A man doesn't lose control and allow his emotions to overcome him. He doesn't let others manipulate him through his emotions, nor fake emotions to manipulate others.

Because humans use emotional displays as a guide, people who readily display emotion can upset the people who care about them.

People are confused when they see someone get emotional over what appears to be a trivial matter. They think "there must be more to this issue," and become frustrated when they can't figure it out. Pieces of the puzzle seem to be missing.

Eventually, hyper-emotional behavior is generally recognized as attention seeking and manipulative. Men don't do this.

Unfortunately, some people just outright fake emotions in their effort to manipulate others. This is what the term "crocodile tears" describes. The emotions they're displaying aren't real. They want people to do something for them, so they pretend.

They fake concern to appear kind. They act sad hoping for charity. Worse still, they might show love, the only emotion that can cause people to give away their everything.

Sometimes emotions are valid, sometimes not. Evaluate carefully those who readily display them. Make sure they aren't attempting to manipulate you. By the same token, be careful with your own emotions. Don't show them easily. You'll stress the people who care about you.

There's another danger as well. If you wear your emotions on your sleeve, you'll be easy to predict. If you're easy to predict, you'll be easy to trick, manipulate or work around.

Your emotions are for you and the people you care about. Don't spread them around. Don't water them down and cheapen them. You wouldn't give your treasure away to strangers, would you?

FINALLY...THE GOOD STUFF

Love

The final chapter.

It may not make a lot of sense, but at the core, being a man is about love.

A man's body is designed — and his behaviors directed — toward providing for loved ones and keeping them safe. A woman understands this on a subconscious level. She wants someone who'll protect her, someone who values her and their children above himself.

While everyone has a built-in need to love, you could argue those who follow the man's code have it in greater measure. A man needs it to fuel both his desire to protect and his willingness to sacrifice. He needs it in exchange for his labor or, ultimately, his life.

So, embrace your love. It's fulfilling like nothing else, but recognize it comes with a price. It's your greatest weakness.

Throughout history, love has been exploited. Forever into the future, this will continue.

FINALLY...THE GOOD STUFF

Love is dangerous: You're at the mercy of those you love. You're chained to them. If they don't love you in return, they can easily manipulate and hurt you, and once in love, you often become blind to their faults. So if possible, be discerning and go into it slow, eyes wide open.

Love has probably killed more people than war. You can be damaged by actions you take on their behalf, or actions they take effecting you. There's also a danger of hurting others, regardless of your intent. While it shouldn't need to be said, never take advantage of someone who loves you.

Despite all the dangers, love is of the utmost importance. Your life will be empty without it. It's bittersweet and often as damning as it is joyous.

I could go on and on about love, but when it captures you, you're beyond reason and most words of wisdom will be forgotten. So, I'll keep it simple: in the end, there's only one thing you need to know: love can give you — and cost you — everything. But no matter what happens, remain willing to pay the entire price, otherwise life loses meaning.

Epilogue — Wrapping it up

You have a choice to make. Maybe not today, but soon.

Will you become a man? If so, you need to make a conscious decision and focus your effort going forward. It's not easy and it won't happen by chance.

You can't control many things in life, but you absolutely can control how you react to them. How you react to things is the essence of your character.

Be the man who evaluates what he does, how he acts and reacts, and learns lessons from both success and failure.

If you're not, setbacks will only wear you down and embitter you.

If you are, you'll grow stronger and stronger over time.

You need to understand your own weaknesses and work on them. You're not perfect, no one is. You have to constantly self-improve by controlling your emotions, improving your body, exercising self-discipline and continuing to learn.

Thankfully, self-improvement is its own reward. You'll know what you've accomplished, even if no one else does. You'll know, and it will fuel your inner fire.

Don't deceive yourself. Be realistic in your self-evaluation. Don't beat yourself up endlessly when you fail or make a big mistake. Own it. Make an accurate assessment of the damage you've caused and figure out how to fix it. If you can't fix it, take your punishment and move on.

Having said that, don't spend a lot of time patting yourself on the back, either. It's fine to take pride in what you accomplish. But don't think once you've done one good thing, people will recognize you and all will be well.

Accomplishments are short-lived and easily forgotten. Most people only consider you as good as the last thing you've done. Realize sometimes it'll take a lot of success to overcome past failures.

The people you need to worry most about impressing are men and women of character. What impresses them is just that: character, or mental and moral strength. You can't bullshit it either, you have to show it.

If you understand this, you'll realize in some cases even when you fail, you can win. Good people won't be interested in your failure as much as how you handled it.

Did you lie about it and try to cover it up? This is the true test. Did you own up to it and take your lumps, despite how difficult or embarrassing it was? The fact you did, will be more important than the failure itself. If you conduct yourself this way, you'll earn the trust of good people.

Likewise, don't worry about what people you don't respect think. Who cares? If they don't know you, why care if they hate you or love you?

Concentrate on making yourself someone of character, worthy of your own respect. You'll then find people come out of nowhere and appreciate who you've become.

Remember "Water finds its level?" Eventually you'll end up surrounded by people just like you. If you never put any effort into improving yourself, you'll be surrounded by similar folks. This will lead to bad times. You'll either find yourself with people who don't try, or people who are so limited in potential they can't accomplish much even when they do.

If you put in the effort to become a man, you'll often find yourself in good company. You'll recognize them and they'll recognize you. You'll be able to trust them and help in their efforts, and they'll do the same. This will prove invaluable.

The military has a saying, "Train hard, fight easy." That means the effort you put into yourself now rewards you down the line.

People notice the strength and competence of men. As a result, men get (often challenging) opportunities others don't. A man's presence says, "Give it to me, I can handle it."

When these opportunities come up, you'll be successful because you've made yourself a man; mentally, morally and physically strong.

The Army taught me a man can walk into a room, wearing the same clothes and having the same haircut as everyone else, and be recognized.

He gets respect from others without saying a word. It's all in the way he interacts, the way he carries himself and what's behind his eyes.

He's recognized as Man.

Final Thought

I imagine most of what I've written is common sense. It's the kind of stuff you read and agree with as a given. Even if you haven't actively considered many of these things, they've been bouncing around in the back of your brain. It's important to know these thoughts are true. Hopefully this book did that and threw in a few new things to think about.

There's a poem, which condenses down almost every truth in this book. It was written in 1895.

IF

IF you can keep your head when all about you

Are losing theirs and blaming it on you,

If you can trust yourself when all men doubt you,

But make allowance for their doubting too;

If you can wait and not be tired by waiting,

Or being lied about, don't deal in lies,

Or being hated, don't give way to hating,

And yet don't look too good, nor talk too wise:

If you can dream - and not make dreams your master;

If you can think - and not make thoughts your aim;

If you can meet with Triumph and Disaster

And treat those two impostors just the same;

If you can bear to hear the truth you've spoken

Twisted by knaves to make a trap for fools,

Or watch the things you gave your life to, broken,

And stoop and build 'em up with worn-out tools:

If you can make one heap of all your winnings

And risk it on one turn of pitch-and-toss,

And lose, and start again at your beginnings

And never breathe a word about your loss;

If you can force your heart and nerve and sinew

To serve your turn long after they are gone,

And so hold on when there is nothing in you

Except the Will which says to them: 'Hold on!'

If you can talk with crowds and keep your virtue,

' Or walk with Kings - nor lose the common touch,

If neither foes nor loving friends can hurt you,

If all men count with you, but none too much;

If you can fill the unforgiving minute

With sixty seconds' worth of distance run,

Yours is the Earth and everything that's in it,

And - which is more - you'll be a Man, my son!

Rudyard Kipling

A classic latchkey kid of the '70s and '80s, J. Allen Hood was raised in Reno, Nevada, the single child of a swing shift casino waitress who wanted him to be the next Fred Astaire. A brief stint in college convinced him to join the military where he spent the next several years on active duty in U.S. Army Special Operations.

After receiving his honorable discharge, he embarked on a series of entrepreneurial and marital adventures which resulted in him losing everything more than once. For the foreseeable future, he will undoubtedly continue to make mistakes, building character along the way.